THIRD
HAND
BOOKS

NOTATION

Jordan Dunn

Thirdhand Books
Columbia, Missouri
3rdhandbooks.com

Published in the United States by:
Thirdhand Books LLC, Columbia, Missouri, 65203
www.3rdhandbooks.com

Library of Congress Cataloging-in-Publication Data on File

ISBN (paperback): 978-1-949344-61-5
ISBN (ePub): 978-1-949344-62-2
1 2 3 4 5

Front cover image: Sketch of Gowing's Swamp, August 23, 1854, by Henry
David Thoreau, as found in *The Writings of Henry David Thoreau*, vol. 4, ed.
Bradford Torrey (Riverside Press, 1906).

Cover design by Lindsey Webb.

Contents

to Laura, Owen, and Liza

. . . the call of a red-winged blackbird as I lift my head to
study the maple buds against the deep green backdrop
of the pine, where the maple buds serve as a bright
visual cue to keep dwelling there even though the source
of the sound remains hidden despite the feeling of
visibility in the blackbird's call or my recognition of its
pattern, like the buzzing robin-like sounds emanating
from the starlings along the creek whom I listened to
this morning, their near-mimicry sly yet resplendent
with the whistled trills for which they are best known:
"the robin's voice seemingly set in the starling filter of
morning, the call's memory as I crouch to examine the
large-flowered bellwort rising from a wreath of trout lily
and hepatica leaves, its yellow flowers drooping at the
end of thin stems, and as I lean further to see if I can
view the inside of the flower without propping it up, my
ear nearly touches the ground as my cheek brushes the
ephemeral leaves from which the bellwort rises; there
must be some greater point to the day than lying
prostrate along the trail, I'm thinking, as I lift my head to
study the boxelder buds sprouting liberally from
beneath the chainsaw cut on the margin of Bear Creek,
the buds are insistent that the roots' energy is expressed
despite the trunk's non-existence, and there is little
evidence I have tried to live a single moment with such
vigor, there are only repetitions of sunlight across the
sand shallows of the creek fading and growing with
intensity as the clouds come and go and I find my
footing upon the trail, where there is nothing profound,
where there is no profundity in the long-beaked sedge,

only this song of visibility to carry further into the day as I remember the various forms of assignment I have given myself to justify the splendid non-being of my mind in relation to the ironwoods" — "no more singing // milkweed seeds floating in and above the / river as I paddled past the forest a huge / cottonwood and the fir beside it // a forest to look at those two floating by // light in the highest west-facing / cottonwood leaves and in the shadows / the same orange in the cones hanging / from the smaller fir tree's upper branches // a yellow leaf floated by suspended steady / and floating below the surface," which patterned for me the mimicry of desire, that is, the desire to go outside and become a thing in a world despite already being a being in the world, the desire to be more than oneself through the observation of the outer world and its way of becoming internalized through this music we bring forward to the moment of composition — a dryad's saddle on the felled boxelder is fresh and therefore deeper brown with less conspicuous spotting than those marks on older specimens, which calls to mind, for some reason, the dark red chevron on the jumpseed leaves newly risen below the mushroom shelf, where supposedly the dryad, the nymph of the forest, would sit in contempla-tion, and though I myself have not seen a nymph I remember my friend's mother who told me she had stopped cutting her lawn because the long grass was more pleasurable for the nymphs that lived in the woods behind her house, and I remember the feeling of not knowing what to say exactly, I mentioned something about fireflies, there were more fireflies in her yard than her neighbor's yard, and she said, yes, the firefly spirits too, it is good for them as well, both the firefly spirits and the nymphs who speak to them, and if I sit out in the clear evening I can hear the murmurs of their conversations, she said, though she didn't know what they were saying exactly, but she was certain the nymphs were speaking to one another and that they were tending to something essential in the forest that we, as humans, don't know how to nurture, so that now, as I reach out to touch the dryad's saddle, I try to parse out her madness from her intuition that we fail to listen carefully enough to powers whose voices grow faint in the confines of our own effacement; that same summer I read *Speak, Memory* and twenty years later it looped back again in Sebald's butterfly man: "I did not know what to reply, but I nodded, and, though everything else around me blurred, I saw that long-forgotten Russian boy as clearly as anything, leaping about the meadows with his butterfly net; I saw him as a messenger of joy, returning from that distant summer day to open his specimen box and release the most beautiful red admirals, peacock butterflies, brimstones and tortoise-shells to signal my final liberation," I have been waiting for the butterfly man all these years though he has yet to arrive, however, the mourning cloaks are out today vis-à-vis Chuck's text in response to the picture I sent of my children balancing on the hackberry log, "look at them kicking up the mourning cloaks," his reference to the butterfly's use of hackberries as host trees, his distinguishing the tree in the photo by the ridgelines and furrows of its unmistakable bark, the text arrived while I had coffee with Cage's book *M* lying open before me: "To finish for Lois programmed / handwritten mushroom / book / including mushroom stories, / excerpts from (mushroom) books, / remarks about (mushroom) hunting, / excerpt from Thoreau's *Journal* / (fungi) / excerpts from Thoreau's *Journal* / (entire) / remarks about: / Life/Art, / Art/Life, / Life/Life, / Art/Art, / Zen, / Current reading, / Cooking (shopping, recipes), / Games, Music mss, Maps, / Friends, / Invention, / Projects, / + / Writing without syntax," Cage's impulse to exclude nothing, to include everything, to create an open frame that functions as a material network served as a model for me during the devastating weeks after Brad died in 2019: "I've started this open notebook approach to my writing in which I am unable to imagine containing things in styles any longer, putting everything together: notes, pictures, sketches, poems, attempts at poems, etcetera, and since moving here last August I've thought about writing a book of letters, a relaxed epistolary as a way out of isolation," I put it down around the time I was helping to organize Brad's memorial service, then life fell into the pandemic, but for me the idea of the perfect book remains thousands of unbound sheets, photographs, and notes spread across a vast table in a skylit warehouse, as this is where I find myself now, studying the text of my walk, the names that fill the pages of the walk, the endless referents opening along the trail as Creeley's lines grow resonant, "words, words / as if all / worlds were there," my attempt to step out of foolishness while remaining in a parallel lightness is not so hard if I lose a grip on expectation, sit by the river, and breathe deeply with the kingfisher; is this Lispector's interval, the moment between moments that I do not remember, the

invisible matter of the interlayered network of being, I
am not so sure, yet further up the trail there is a field
overtaken by sumac that forms a savanna where I'm
greeted by what appears to be a *Psychomorpha*, a black
moth, a daytime flyer, small, seemingly a butterfly but
decidedly not a butterfly, it moves on above the sumac
then down toward a juniper: "Into that arena of radi-
ance, moths would come drifting out of the solid
blackness around me, and it was in that manner, upon
that magic sheet, that I took a beautiful *Plusia* (now
Phytometra) which, as I saw at once, differed from its
closest ally by its mauve-and-maroon (instead of
golden-brown) forewings, and narrower bractea mark
and was not recognizably figured in any of my books,"
thinking of how Ratcliffe opens *More Rocks*, "cloud,
suddenly / there is one and // after that two, / how
mitosis // in cells goes on," wondering whether the
perception of the clouds shifted during Ratcliffe's hike in
the Sierra Nevada in 1994, whether he saw one cloud at
first that then proved to be two, like the cell that is one
but then becomes two, then becomes four, "stopping to
look / down at it, I // who also stop / thinking this, that
// is, what might be / in syllables // meant by this, this
/ being the end," as though there is a necessary differ-
ence between this moment of perception and the reality
of the clouds, their division and the relation between
memory and the access to memory in the clouds of
time, not a narrative, I remember, but a pathway
between other pathways with no good reason for my
having chosen one or the other, such that when I look
back through a thicket of time I grow satisfied not by the
plain texture of my life's story, not by the secure

structure of its becoming, but by the sheer unreliability
of its patterning, as if my self divides but I remain
unaware of its division until I return to my starting
point — the call of a red-winged blackbird as I lift my
head to study the maple buds against the deep green
backdrop of the pine, several photos atop a stack of
books illuminating the present moment along with
Rick's manuscript, *A Duration*, the moments I appear
there as Jordan, and when L or Lewis or L or Lisa
appear in the same passage I desire completely to be
transported inside the text, to take up residence there,
the way one may for a long time stare into a photograph
and actuate the contours of its prior reality that
somehow brushes against the present with such
startling intensity the interval evaporates beyond the
serviceberry flowering on the hillside above me . . .

. . . the flair of red on the kinglet's crown is finally visible
among the chokecherry flowers as the bird flits on a
low branch near the forest floor above the emerging
green leaves of cutleaf coneflower and stinging nettle,
"From the first, not a thing there is, except what you
have made out of your own illusive mind," as I lower my
binoculars the cherry flower scent is brightly forgiving,
the kinglet's position there with its ruby crown flashing
among the inflorescence until a jumbled song emanates
from the hackberry above and mixes with the slightest
of whitewater sounds rising from the river that runs
over a rippled bank of small stones adjacent a long, low
islet that splits the river's shallow water in two before
its confluence downstream: "The duality of the subject
and object is gone – which is called the seeing into
self-nature / It is evident that this seeing into self-nature
is not an ordinary seeing, in which there is a duality of
one who sees and that which is seen," here is a gift to my
insignificance, I'm thinking, as I pluck a thorn from the
honey locust and test it to my thumb, it would be easy
to draw blood under the swallows chasing around the
canopy's edge, those birds, it was once thought, who
disappear below the waters of English lakes to hibernate
for the winter, as it is a dream today to hibernate at this
point in my life, to enter a burrow of sleep and undo the
rigors of winter until sunshine emits enough energy for
the taking, although, what does it mean to desire hiber-
nation in the springtime as I stand before the kinglet
and its shelter of chokecherry flowers, to think this while
I witness the fading of my recollection's intensity and

make the decision to not write it down, to reconstruct
it at a later time, writing now "tree swallow, northern
flicker, fox sparrow," reaching twenty-seven species on
this April morning — "this present tense that refuses no
one, this present tense that refuses no one, this present
tense that refuses no one," I repeat the line found in the
middle of Rick's manuscript, it feels like an ethics of
presence compared to my own teetering at the edge of a
standstill, "this present tense that refuses no one," that is,
what tunes itself to being and memory and the wave-like
flux between them, get back to that, I'm imagining, so
I give myself permission to move into the poem, and
because the poem includes me and my friends and the
arrangement of death or our proximities to mortality,
I begin to read again: "Brad turned a tottering circle
clutching the dog, Trapper, to his chest on slippery
slanted moss cliff path 50 feet above the rocks and water
he didn't worry or fall he scrambled up to the proper
path / Jordan turned around and crossed again the gap
that made him feel death close / Later I heard mourning
in the bird songs he performed," then I lean forward and
return to my own writing: "how fear still encircled my
body as I undressed and tested the temperature of the
water, how as I eased myself down into the rock pool
the adrenaline that brought me to that point must have
been, at some level, mixed with the mist that was rising
before my eyes, covering my body, and fogging my view
of the very cliff from which I had almost slipped to my
death," the silence I let float there between cycles of
song that were, for Rick, full of mourning, "wee-see-
wee-see-wit-a-wit-a-wit, wee-see-wee-see-wit-a-wit-
a-wit, wee-see-wee-see-wit-a-wit-a-wit," I want to be

surrounded by the text entirely, to inhabit it, because
there is the moment prolonged of Brad's being alive, not
simply the memory of his aliveness, so my repetition last
night of Rick's line produced my desire for the present
moment to feel just like that, unrefused, and my sudden
recognition that, in the act of composition, I had learned
to refuse my grief, and because there is no longer any
way to reassure those turbulent parts of my self that
were, for over twenty years, stabilized by my friendship
with Brad, I have also learned to refuse those most
basic elements of my past that offer shared proof of our
friendship, as though any evidence of his reassurance
merely accentuates my anxiety — I nibble on a little
waterleaf pinched from a plant beside the trail, update
my list of birds, return to the task of photographing the
property border signs to make into a visual poem, "Park
Boundary Respect Private Property," but the deer are
free to loosely wander around the signs toward their
embankment by the river: "a narrowing dense collec-
tion of hoofprints leads to a shallow crossing of Walnut
Creek below Greenwood Park, where the floodplain is
rich with rudbeckia leaves and the emerging flowerheads
of bluebells, I follow the hoofprints to a sandbar, look
for wood ducks, hope for the pileated woodpecker's
wild posture among the mammoth sycamores, and
the peents of the mudsnipe remind me of the marsh
in Madison where I would sit on the gravel road alone
in April twilight while the mudsnipes performed their
mating dance in the sky, the sundown chill on my nose,
not so much has changed, I remember, as I linger on the
sandbar in the creek, the intentions remain the same
even though the perception of them has grown distorted

by an undefinable pain that is regulated by the wafting
sweetness of the plum flower's position along the bank
in relation to the wood ducks dabbling, not relieved,
the pain, but clarified, therefore it flows to a part of me
that is agreeably inaccessible in this spring air; what was
it I read about 'no-mind' on the island where my canoe
rested overturned on a sandy shore, something about
the measurement of pain being proportional to the ego
and its tremors among this reality that is actually an illu-
sion, what a bummer, I remember thinking, that none
of this is real, not even my face reflected in the unsteady
mirror of the gently lapping lake, nor the water striders
skimming across the retreating image of my reflection as
I stand up and return to my camp among the pines" . . .

. . . "The aim of this writing / is to show that / I does
not disappear / Even when I disappear I / does not
disappear," Lewis pours cream into his coffee, stirs it
with a small spoon, and as he looks intently into the
yellow cup a yellow warbler rises into the lilac at the
back of the garden, "a pair of yellows," I write into my
notebook, "there's an insistence upon friendship in the
circulation of the text," like our return alongside the
green dragon flower when I asked, is it another, and
Lewis replied it was the same as the one we passed
previously, as he had taken note of the dead hollowed
tree limb by our feet in whose cavity we watched a large
millipede curl before it disappeared beneath a collec-
tion of leaves, but it is another flower in a certain way,
he said, because I only recognize its placement, not its
particular flower-ness, which made me feel safe, causing
me to later write: "the cleft leaflets of the green dragon
appear as two despite being one, jack-in-the-pulpit
below as I bend lower to examine the flower's spathe,
discovering the spadix there beneath the tongued lid
hiding, 'darkness to ripple / the line of spring'" — "Dear
Jordan, I found myself staring at the bookshelf late this
afternoon in the heat and settled on Henry James's *The
Golden Bowl* because Murnane refers to the preface,
I started there, and found myself thinking of you for
several reasons: 'the idea, that is, of the aspect of things
or the combination of objects that might, by a latent
virtue in it, speak for its connexion with something in
the book, and yet at the same time speak enough for
its odd or interesting self,'" as there is no clear way to

understand what begins in the book and what begins in
life, especially when we are inside of the book, or this
is what I understood by Rick's note in relation to my
present response as I turn toward the sound of Lewis
tapping a spoon against the rim of his coffee cup, the
sound feels somehow loving to me among our two or
multiple selves joined through friendship's arrangement
on the page, "to not endear the writing to its future
legibility but only to its current, compositional legi-
bility, and in that case there are no boundaries," let's
pause for a moment, I say, as I go inside to get *Word
Rain*, "I appear on a page which would otherwise be
blank, I appear on a page which would otherwise be
blank," and the start of Lewis's book before it became a
book, "Even when I disappear I / does not disappear,"
a decorative void floats in the ephemeral slip of air that
follows the warbler's flight up into the lilac, which is
how the sentence began before it was revised and placed
above the comment about the poem's circulations in
the warm spring air, so I read aloud to Lewis my idea
of his idea of reading as he leans back to take in the
garden: "One way to read a book is to carry it around
all day but not to open it, and since I have tried this
kind of reading I can say it is true, as long as you carry
the book very close to your body and remember its
power is beside you, your subconscious will read the
book and you will absorb the text, but the text will not
arrive in a familiar form because it will be layered and
topographical; having adjusted to the rhythms of your
day and the circumstances in which you find yourself
with the text, its legibility will prove difficult, perhaps
unreadable, but nonetheless, you will have received the

book's secrets and you will have understood all of the space between the words, the space around the words, the space inside and around the letters whose marks only partly compose the words, then you will know that the text is mostly empty and is understood by its emptiness as much as its mark on the page, and this is why keeping the book closed is a remarkable form of reading, because it honors the general emptiness of the page and therefore the emptiness of the book, and this is why I align the text with my own emptiness, for it is at this point I most resemble the book and therefore most resemble myself," as Rick's note about *The Golden Bowl* continues: "That this metaphor describes so exactly my own literal experience all last winter of postholing to the bluff in deep snow, in or sometimes between my own tracks, in some way knits the two together, like your poem that consists only of walking, that publishes itself, and even, as James says, revises itself day after day"...

5-28-21   Portland, OR

. . . "trees of heaven, a row of ginkgoes, junk maple, a
pear tree, three neatly pruned apple trees, the fragrant
poised salvia at the garden gate beyond the artichokes,
two rows of green cabbage, the prolific fruit of strawber-
ries reddening the garden border," yesterday afternoon,
only off the plane for thirty minutes, I gathered snap
peas, contemplated the hop vines that had overtaken
the chain link fence, and I understood very little about
myself other than the feeling of my back relaxing as it
was no longer constrained by my position in seat 23B,
unable to lean left or right, the airplane noise fading as I
closed my eyes and turned up *Landwerk* on my head-
phones, a transport to the analog sound of 78-record-
groove static mixed with rhythms of filtered guitar and
a fog horn in the near distance, the melody loops and
loops but does not disintegrate in its ambience, the way
one story gives way to memory which then gives way
to memory's story, how the last time I sat at this desk
nearly two years ago overlooking the same garden I was
organizing Brad's business papers only six days after his
sudden death, struggling to assist his partner, Nicky,
who had no direct access to his accounts, my bed for
that week a camping pad and Brad's sleeping bag on
the floor of the office where a nightmare twitch awak-
ened me to a metallic taste in my mouth like a bloody
playground lip from childhood, unable now to hear the
music even though the record spins the constellation of
its statics, returning me to the desk and my description
of the garden: "clipping parsley, arugula, basil, gathering
eggs from the coop while eyeing the radish bed, a spliff

reopens time as Luke arrives from downtown in his work van, the question of who will tend to the chickens and water the garden when we head to the coast" — definitely a nautilus, Nicky and I agree after staring for some time at the figure of a sea creature sketched in the tidal sand that we stumbled upon in the late-night fog, I'm feeling a little nauseous, I admit to her, just don't grind your teeth, that means you're getting close, she says, in reference to her own habitual response to the dose kicking in, and as we walk up to dry sand and sit down Luke heads in the opposite direction toward the crashing waves made invisible by the thickness of the fog, and as I huddle up with my chest toward my thighs I can feel the dampness of the air has already descended upon my clothing as Luke's figure grows faint and disappears into the haze, I rock there a moment, trying to determine where my mind is heading, the yellow sleeve of Nicky's rain jacket tied onto her backpack registers a photograph I stared into earlier in the morning, in which she wears the same jacket at the edge of the ocean as Brad embraces her: "I light a joint and discover its ember tracing across my line of sight, my body loses its tightness and my stomach begins to calm as I run my hand through my hair then run both hands up and down my thighs, I'm feeling very good now, I say to Nicky, whose smile in reply acknowledges her own movement beyond a shared threshold, and after we finish the joint we wonder openly about Luke who has been out of sight for a long time, or what feels like a long time, so I hand Nicky my headlamp and she walks toward the ocean, her figure, too, grows faint and disappears into the crashing wave fog, 'as if there were no release from the darkness that is a good way beyond this world and which feels to exist outside of time'" — the crow's shadow moves across the square of sunshine cast upon the wall by the skylight, the sound of several crows prowling the rooftop as the cedar limbs gather wind, through a diamond opening in the high quincunx fence I can see the Pacific's horizon partially obscured by the cedar's branches, where a spotted towhee calls repeatedly before it returns to a sickly shrub surrounded by European beachgrass; a message arrives from the Midwest that describes an odd encounter with a distempered blackbird, in reply I send a video of the dry beach sand streaming over the wet tidal sand, forming miniature dunes on the windward side of the small, smooth stones that have been pulled toward the ocean with the ebb of the waves, and the towhee's persistent call reminds me of my walks along Wreck Beach at UBC, where they sang frequently in mid-June, and where I found an abandoned wetsuit alongside a weather-beaten book titled, *The Introvert's Advantage: How to Thrive in an Exterior World* . . .

. . . "a rain shower dimples the river as I put on my coat
and upturn its hood, a breeze pushes my kayak hori-
zontal to the current before I grab my paddle, right my
course, and drift over to Nicky who is on the lookout for
impatiens near the shore, we find their leaves but not
their flowers mixed in with stinging nettle, water parsley,
and poison oak; a few minutes ago Nicky found a
dragonfly for little Fox who watched it alight on the tip
of his finger, the sound of the small waterfall spilling
down into the river surrounded by wreaths of maiden
hair fern mixed with Fox's laughter, and I was struck by
the memory of climbing with Brad to the second tier of
Pup Creek Falls in 2018, the incessant roar of the water
as it fell, on its first drop, 200 feet from the high ridge
above, and I couldn't help but wonder what it would feel
like to drop with the water from that great height, to
somehow be recoverable afterwards, as a body
breathing, to get up and walk away as I did a few days
prior at the creek that flows down from the hot springs
where I swam out into the plunge pool, dove under
toward the tumbling current of the much smaller
waterfall, to feel the power of the churning current turn
my body over and over, then to escape that feeling of my
own will, on my own accord, as I later described it to
Luke in his living room while we sat listening to *The
Disintegration Loops*, several camellia blossoms floated in
a bowl of water, and I remarked that he had brought the
outside inside as he flicked the wheel on his lighter with
his thumb, guided the flame to his joint, and grew
pensive as often happens in the small extension of

thought that rides along with inhalation, I guess you're
right, he said, as he exhaled, then he lifted the bowl up
slightly and set it down so as to stir the water, which
caused the camellia blossoms to turn about, brushing
their fuchsia petals together" — reviewing my notes
from our paddle on the river: "wildflower list from the
Clackamas: ookow, Cascade beardtongue, arnica, water
parsley, seep monkeyflower, shining crane's bill,
American brooklime, Pacific ninebark, stonecrop, Nicky
found a dragonfly for little Fox beneath the waterfall that
runs down into the river beside a small, sandy landing
full of stinging nettle and English ivy," I pause to think
through Endi's comment from the day before as we
rounded the top of Mount Tabor, notes, Endi said,
whatever it takes to keep the practice going, my remem-
bering now that as we walked up through the park I
described plans for my photos of sand patterns from
Oceanside, how I wanted make prints extracted from
the ephemeral situation of the tidal patterns, and Endi
stopped me to explain that the seaweed photos in her
chapbook were from Oceanside, and I said that even
though this seems like a noticeable coincidence it is
probably my own time spent working on her chapbook
that caused me to begin thinking about the patterns in
the sand, that it was no coincidence at all but quite
literally a kind of transference — a hammock hangs
from the walnut tree, an ill walnut beside the healthier
walnut, the sun rises from behind the cherry tree
slanting light across the table where I type, my hands'
shadows on the keyboard, a silhouette of a desert tree
printed on my coffee cup, a cowboy with his pony, the
name Joe Reno set against the sunset scene, which

contrasts with the verdant Oregon white oak leaves
above my head, and these few descriptions revive my
sense of home, otherwise feeling a little adrift among my
travels, my lack of obvious mission, trying to turn the
minor events of my day into a practice of writing, their
small commotions that swirl interior to the subject, I am
simply a person who changes place, and the locusts
across the street remind me of the floodplains of Iowa,
which by now must be vining with poison ivy, wild
grape, and the beautiful leaves of moonseed; on our
walk last week or the week before, I described to Laura
that I love the name moonseed because it possesses a
soft-looking leaf within it, as if a child named the plant
in a moment of self-recognition, realizing now that other
plant and fungi names involve the planets: three-seeded
mercury, Venus flytrap, earthstar, *The Rings of Saturn*, I
do not understand why I would again choose a novel
about the dark revolutions of our planet, its human
population's predisposition for annihilation, why I
would bring this book with me when I knew I would be
sleeping in a dead friend's house, carrying plenty of my
own darkness upon waking; yesterday I escaped the
95-degree heat by lying under maples and reading about
the slow destruction of Dunwich in the fourteenth
century, finally transitioning to field guide entries about
American dune grass before a sudden memory of spider-
wort bordering the front stoop of our Madison home
caused me to stand up and stretch my legs, my book
would be about grief, I thought, dissolution scarred by
the repetition of its avoidance, my unwillingness to face
the future undoing the composition's present tense by
configuring a rufous-sided hummingbird, for example,

resting on a telephone line above yellow beach lupine,
"no private viewing, no public viewing," wondering now
as the sun climbs above the cherry tree if orbit is a
decent metaphor for grief, how the loss becomes a
satellite pain that orbits the subject, gradually breaking
down into smaller and smaller constituent pieces that do
not dissipate but merely become less visible in the
half-light — Luke and Nicky pull up and we begin
arranging ladders, containers, and five-gallon buckets to
pick tart cherries, soon Nicky is up in the tree sitting on
a branch lowering her small container of cherries to
Luke who deposits them in the five-gallon bucket, is it
worth it, Nicky asks, to drive back and pick up the
fourteen-foot orchard ladder in order to reach the
topmost branches brimming with bunches of deep red
fruits; attached to a high limb, the rope swing drifts in
the wind while the sky continues clearing, there is a
symptom I carry while I climb the ladder and smile, it
dissipates in the leaves that brush my shoulders as I
climb even higher toward the brightest fruits — Luke
saved the mint-condition record of translated haiku for
three years to listen first with me, and as we lay back on
the couch I closed my eyes and gradually descended
into a near-dream as images of autumn leaves, mountain
lakes, cedars, starlight, and a wandering crow's plum tree
brought me first to the Adirondacks and then to the
feeling of walking toward my record player as it sat on a
cabinet in our home in Madison four years ago,
windows open to the early June wind, all of my life
regulated by a different pain, the image of that record
spinning next to the sunny south-facing window while
Luke's record spun descriptions of a waveless, still lake

and the geese who mirror deeply their reflections in the
moonlight, it is impossible to know their relation but
nonetheless I am pulled deeper into a near-sleep, into
those pasts that feel inaccessible by their sheer distance,
and the accumulations of habit's daily detritus are
momentarily closer than their successors or even the
punch of the present tense — the trip is near its end so
I've sat down to piece together several fragments of
reading, not books but the reading of friendships over
time and my rhythm of visits to this city, returning by
car or bicycle or plane, the familiar look of the foothills,
city parks, white-capped Mount Hood in the distance,
the sensation of being pulled between two lives no
longer one I can relate to, simply the contented pull of
gravity back to the Midwest; there's an absence in the
seasons here that I cannot wrap my mind around, it
seems to keep the shape of life from being hardened off
around the edges, time is less defined and death feels
both close and far away, like the overturned SUV on
Route 6 heading back from the coast, no clear indication
as to why the vehicle crashed on a straightaway, no skid
marks, it was turned over on its roof with a worried
group of people huddled around a rescue crew at the
end of a long driveway, recalling a similar accident
coming out of the coast range in 2018 that Brad and I
passed on the way back from Astoria, a head-on
collision, blood spattered on a shattered windshield, the
jaws of life running while police officers herded traffic
into a single lane — I follow the shoreline to a tunnel
that leads onto a hidden, cliff-backed beach accessible
only at low tide, there is a moment when the light from
the opposite end is not enough to guide my body over

the driftwood that was strewn across the tunnel by
violent winter storms, I move forward step by step to
feel my footing until there is enough light to reach the
tunnel's end and I emerge onto the secluded beach, "in a
high slow turning of gulls / gliding and hanging /
dropping and rising / joy samples its levels," and
although I know joy is the feeling I am walking toward
there is no reaching it except in the poem; several
pelicans are fishing out by the largest sea stacks, they
hover above the whitecaps before diving down fast into
the water, a mist hovers at eye level across the beach as I
step from rock to rock while the wet sand is washed
regularly by the rising and retreating waves, the over-
powering sound of the waves crashing against the rock
startles me as a rush of water sneaks up over my feet
then retreats, it is a small, gilded fear trembling in the
sunlight that is now arching over the cliff to clear the fog
as I reenter the tunnel — I startle awake and move off
the couch to the patio, where browned camellia petals
form a ring around the lowest branches, several blos-
soms are still apparent among the succulent-like leaves
as the sky's overcast countenance provides small breaks
of sunlight; Ari the cat has made his way to my lap
because it is cool and damp in the house, a gust of wind
pivots his attention toward the window as we both
glance out at the street, where a lone walker pushes a
shopping cart loaded with what appears to be junk-picks
wrapped in all manner of plastic and garbage bags, and
even from this distance I can hear the wheels of the cart
grind hard against pebbled gravel that has been cast up
from the unpaved shoulder . . .

7-1-21   Ames, IA

. . . I pick squash bug nymphs from the young butternut
plant, remove clusters of bronze eggs from the under-
sides of the leaves, and the story begins as my eye follows
an ant along the cedarwood garden border until it
disappears into straw mulch below a tiny forest of wood
sorrel, "I'm trying to seize the fourth dimension of this
instant-now so fleeting that it's already gone because it's
already become a new instant-now that's also already
gone," I fetch a field knife to harvest arugula and beet
greens, and as I kneel down to cut the tallest plants in
the row I notice how clean the leaves are from yester-
day's rain, the leaves had lain down upon the straw
after the shower only to rise up again in the morning's
sun that now streams through the kitchen window as I
open the patio door and step inside, fill up a canning jar
with water to hold tall stems of spearmint that will keep
well in the ambient air for several days or more: "It so
happens that the primary thought – as an act of thought
– already has a form and is more easily transmitted to
itself, or rather, to the very person who is thinking it;
and that is why – because it has a form – it has a limited
reach," the floors of the kitchen are sandy against my
bare feet, the sand having found its way from the porch
into the kitchen when I unpacked the tents near the
door in order to air them out on a taut line stretching
across the yard, and although we did not camp on the
beach our daily wanderings carried us there, we brought
back sand in our pockets and in our shoes, gradually
it accumulated in the tent corners, and now it is here
under my feet in the kitchen 450 miles from Lake

Superior, a small deposit or shift in the composition of
things, and the feeling of the sand registers the memory
of photographing sensitive fern along the boardwalk
across the bog leading to a stand of jack pine hot in the
sun: "how far to the beach, Owen asks, very close now
I say, as I feel the wind off the great lake cool the air we
both sit down to take off our shoes, and even though
the lakeshore is not yet in sight the trail has become
increasingly sandy, this sense of feeling the presence of a
thing despite not seeing it, a feeling in the air resembles
a history only I may possess, and there is a disappoint-
ment that follows me as the sound of the wind in the
pines mixes with the rush of the waves breaking and it
becomes impossible to determine which sounds come
from the treetops or which sounds come from the
whitecap waves of the lake" — wayfinding, that's what
I'm thinking, as Andy describes tying a thin cord from
point to point in the woods that borders the pond, then
blindfolding his students to have them follow the length
of the cord slowly, carefully, touching the plants and the
trees and the ground to find their way, even following
the cord over downed trees across muddy low places,
he explains that some students moved especially slowly
in order to feel every being along their path, the leaves
of the glade mallows and the bark of the oaks and the
polypore mushrooms growing on silver maples, artist's
conks, Andy says, as we dip our bare feet into Lake
Wingra from the edge of the dock, how's writing, he
asks, and I try to describe this feeling at the moment
of inscription, that it's a feeling to study, to understand
more, not the intention of the composition, but the
fiction of my being present in the face of all possible

outcomes, the pleasurable constraint of maintaining
a line of events and interjections that are not precon-
ditioned but arise at the moment of composition, or
appear to, because I'm still uncertain, I say, what is
ordering the images' attachments to each other and what
is causing some of them to brighten enough to stand out
against the shifting background of their origin ...

. . . I sit up in bed and listen to the cicada's call fade as
night falls into a katydid rhythm, a cricket undertone
humming into the memory of spring, "where deer paths
led in three directions through the buckthorn grove
and I chose one, then doubled back and tried another,
searching for an entrance into the marsh," I turn on a
lamp and move to the desk covered by a collection of
letters, photographs, and notebooks that accompanied
me an hour ago, and as I reopen Mariko's letter I'm
reminded of the notes she would leave on my doorstep
during college and the walks we would take across town
that would end beneath a canopy of magnolia flowers:
"Dear Mariko, I have not written a single word since I
read your letter eleven days ago, I think I've resided in
that space of wordlessness, the way words fail in our
grieving that you aptly imagined as a blank space in your
notebook / It is still unbelievable that your brother,
Charlie, and our friends from that night fifteen years
ago, Sharon and Brad, have all died within such a short
period, and that grief is now both confused and ines-
capable / How to describe that feeling of being unable
to control the darkness when it settles inside you / The
first night I was back in Portland, Nicky gave me one
of Brad's sleeping bags to lie down in, and I must have
fallen asleep for a few hours because the situation of my
surroundings was familiar and warm to me, but some-
time before dawn I shot awake, stood up, and felt like
my body was about to tear itself in half, like there was
sharp metal inside of me that wanted to panic and flail
over and over until nothing was left" — "a light breeze

moves through the hemlock boughs while I boil water
for coffee and watch the lake glisten in the morning sun,
a harvest spider rests on my foot before I guide it back
into the wood chips near the fire ring, robins overhead,
chickadees, the noise of a zipper from the tent, stuff
sacks rustling as Owen gets dressed for the day, I see his
feet appear from under the rain fly as he slips on hiking
shoes before I write: 'reading last night at the campfire
about the method of loci, how monks would build
elaborate palaces in their minds to organize vast stores
of information, walking room to room to recover what-
ever was needed: a list of medicinal plants, the names
of angels, entire texts committed to memory, how these
architectures reminded me of my need to possess a
narrative structure for my past that holds at bay the
shifting currents of the present'" — "Dear Jordan, it may
have been the night that Mark and much of the party
got naked and wrote poetry on their bodies, I feel like
there were a lot of tambourines and the night just kept
going like we came for dinner and then just stayed and
stayed and at some point the memory fades and I open
my eyes and I am waking up on the couch, cradled by
Brad, and I saw these doves on the ledge of a window
on the building that was quite close to your apartment
right outside the living room window, and those cooing
doves have stuck in my mind as a manifestation of a holy
moment like a drop of water in my mind" — "sunflecks
on sugar maple saplings, 'yellow birch, cumulus' written
in pencil, that would be a nice place to have a cabin,
Owen says, of the meadow where the cabin once
stood, he reads a novel as I write 'one blue jay feather,
doll's eyes of the baneberry, feather with a violet sheen,

bunchberries, several muddy crossings of marigold streams, Clintonia, the smallmouth bass caught with difficulty who had two old hooks in its mouth, a touring canoe sunlit with life vests drying on the yoke, it is not such a distance from the heart to the image in the mind, and at least some tragic side of the picture partakes 'to give the whole of life through this darker medium,' its bright and splendid lights become thus lurid / Buoy- antly it floated, and now weighed, it sinks gently / high in down thistledown descends / buoyantly it floated high / when it but comes down it descends buoyantly into the serene evening // do gales shake windfalls from thy tree'" — it isn't enough, I'm thinking, as I turn from my desk, head quietly down the hallway to the front door, slip on my shoes and walk out into the August night where the sweetness of flower-ripened air mixes with my thoughts of reading Mariko's letter; the neighbor's wind chimes ring lightly while I make my way toward the creek, where haloes of fireflies flicker over the ballfield as I cross the street to walk among them, then along the floodplain, where the grasses are thick and dark: "Dear Jordan, sometimes I feel angry with time, as if it were a thing, angry for the way it moves, 'Incompletándonos de todo' (chipping away at our whole), I feel not only grief, which I will just leave a big, empty space here for, since I lack the ability to put it into words, but I also feel fear and loss for myself, like this strange angel piece of me is disappearing," a settled coolness rests in the damp air among the reed grass and thick red osier shrubs, I lay down beside the path, listen to the soft wind play the petioles of the quaking leaves high up in the towering cottonwood, where a resonance between the rustling leaves and the starlight escapes my insomnia, and the lines I read earlier in the night sift my thoughts through several filters of memory: "extinction follows us // whether we mean it to / or not"...

. . . the river ice is thick enough to walk upon and clear
enough to see the flow of water in the deepest channels
that follow the sweeping cut banks of the river's bends,
the meanders, I suppose, to match our wandering
upstream among boxelder and black willow debris; I
stop and bend down to look at the river flowing beneath
the ice, an elm leaf caught between twigs exhibits a kind
of pulse, it waves left then right and back again as the
small pressures of the water move it side to side, and as
I look closer I see that the stem is caught in an inter-
locking nest of twigs pushed up against a heavier branch
half-embedded in the sand, this must be the point, I say,
and Laura asks, what, do you want to turn around, as the
sun breaks through a gap in the January sky we follow
a deer trail up the sandbar then back into the woods
— on our Zoom call Rick read his poem that describes
his taking a picture of me as I stood beside Mill Creek,
his assuming I was inspecting the creek but when he
climbed down the short bluff to meet me he discovered
that I had been looking at a deer skull that sat beside
the water, my description beside the creek about the
time I found a scavenged deer in winter whose posture
had been left intact, curled up below coralberries at the
edge of a different creek, a mixture of skeleton and fur
and skinless flesh, somehow left whole while also being
pieced apart, its ribcage void, its hooves untouched,
the sound of the creek where it flowed under a tangle
of old barbed wire, Rick's writing about my description
of the scavenged deer after he joined me beside the
creek, and my listening to him read his writing about

listening to my story, the moment now when I write
that, having turned away from binding the accordion
book on which is printed, "a rustle beyond honeysuckle:
14 deer, / I count, nibbling forbs in the / floodplain,
and no sign of ginseng / up here in the photograph /
its unwinding half-life, a place in the / fantasy measure-
ment of memory," perhaps it is location I am trying to
move away from, or the situation of standing still, not
wanting the page to stall time or halt its progression, to
hide within its unfolding or the binding of its becoming:
"the accordion book form is potentially infinite as
long as the bookmaker continues to hinge the sections
together, it can be read in one's lap like a regular book or
support itself upright when it is only partially extended,
resembling a series of connected VVVVs from above,
or if viewed from the side, a mountain range rotated
horizontally, peak to peak pointed toward the horizon
opposed to the sky, or it can be arranged in a star shape
so that the covers meet and the pages look toward one
another, such that the book reads itself in panoramic
form, and it may even be left alone that way, so that the
text faces itself and becomes invisible through the act of
mirroring" — there was a moment when the psilocybin
was kicking in and we were protected in the arboretum
by a copse of pines, you never finished telling me about
Sartre, Mike said, and suddenly I felt lost, not only by
my inability to recall *Being and Nothingness* or to finish
my ideas surrounding some aspect of it, but by the
uncanny feeling that I was suddenly hollow, and it was a
feeling that a cigarette would not fix, so we lay down on
a bed of pine needles secluded from the world, feeling
for a while like we were dying, or Mike did, at least, as

he told me, I think I am dying now, please tell my mom I love her, and something about Mike's dying made a part or all of me feel the same way as I faded toward my own death, causing me to share a story about my mother, how she would cross-country ski with me in Michigan under the pines when I was young, how at certain points the boughs would hang low as we glided through them as though through a tunnel, and it made me feel very safe skiing those sections of the trail, in particular the needles of the white pines were gentle and welcoming, I would sometimes reach out and hold onto them at the top of a rise, then Mike asked me, what kind of pines are these, I don't know if it matters right now, I replied, they are just what we need, then he told me a story about his own mother, and that was how we came out of it, returning to the promise of the late May afternoon, the trip ending on the porch of my apartment as I read to him Kyger's reflection on Spicer: "That's when you understand that words have their own independent existence / They say what they want to / you are just the medium, the funnel for the words to go through / They have their own lineage, returning through you," then reading Spicer's letter to Blaser: "Two inconsequential things can combine together to become a consequence / This is true of poems too / A poem is never to be judged by itself alone / A poem is never by itself alone / This is the most important letter you have ever received . . ."

. . ."The sudden brief early morning breeze, the first
indication of a day's palpability, stays high in the trees,
while flashing silver and green the leaves flutter, a bird
sweeps from one branch to another, the indistinct
shadows lift off the crumpled weeds / It always gets
darkest before it gets absolutely black / If there's nothing
out the windows look at books / There is tension in
the connecting string," I set Hejinian's book down and
peer out the window into the yard where a fox squirrel
has positioned itself on a low-hanging branch in Kay's
maple, I tend to the squirrel's image in my mind before
it climbs up into the crown of the maple and leaps onto
the bur oak, the refrains of Akira Rabelais have cycled
back to their beginning such that a single voice rises
from the silence before it is joined by a second voice
that aligns in mourning but not in time, "You should
know that there is One Mind only, and besides this
there is not an atom of anything you can claim to be
your own," a trace memory of driving through the night-
dark rain inside the same choral cycles of lamentation,
shifting between uncertainties about the future and the
dream that offered an interflow of memory in which
I was playing pool with Brad at a dive bar while also
planning a party with him that would be staged in an
old-growth forest on the coast, a system of tree houses
we would build ourselves, with hanging bridges between
them so the guests would never touch the ground for
the entire party; the two of us hike midday on a high
ridge in the Cascades just beyond the Saint Helens blast
zone, the trail cuts through a wildflower meadow and

eventually descends to Deadman's Lake, which woke
me, I believe, as I dreamed the letters of the name routed
on the weather-worn trail sign just as they appear in
an actual photograph of Brad while backpacking the
Goat Mountain trail in August 2011, or my imagina-
tion of the Deadman's Lake sign as I stood beside it
to photograph our friends after we struck camp — I
have taken one of the plates of shale that I collected in
December from the sandbar along the Raccoon River
and placed it on a sheet of copy paper where it rests on
my desk beside a micrometer that measures its thinnest
point at twenty-eight thousandths of an inch, similar in
thickness to a sheet of handmade cover paper, and as I
again pick up the piece of shale its lightness surprises
me despite having measured its thinness only a moment
ago, I feel determined to find a way to bind together all
of the seven plates of shale I carefully separated from
the original block with a putty knife, the act of sliding
the knife into the fissures between the plates, the deep
history of their depositions, to break it apart, to bind
it together again, these movements with the pages of
a book, it being closed or open, looking for a middle
space that describes the period between reading and not
reading, Gilbert White's *The Natural History of Selborne*,
the copy I purchased was printed so long ago the binder
did not trim the fore-edge of the signatures, meaning
that the book, despite being over a hundred years old,
was unread, or, since being "uncut" proved that it was
unread, such that turning page five meant that pages six
& seven were enclosed inside the fold and one turned
immediately to page eight, and therefore pages six &
seven were unreadable unless the book was set upright

and I pushed one folio into a cylinder, like a tunnel, in
order to peer down into the chamber of text, so I read
White's book with a short, serrated knife on my desk,
cutting along each fold when it came time to reveal the
interior-facing pages, thus one became two, each single
leaf now forming two pages, "Reason looks for two,
then arranges it from there" — "Al, burn these," was the
extent of Niedecker's note to her husband with direc-
tions to destroy her correspondence after her death,
that's true love, I think, that he went through with it and
made a bonfire of her papers even though we consider it
a deep loss, or the people who study her life in rela-
tionship to her poems consider it so, and after I close
the book and set it down I walk in circles around the
living room while I look for a starting place, then I open
the book back up and page through the first chapter,
it is beginning, I think, as I sit down to write this, as if
there's a method that determines the writing's origin
and measures the pulse of its text, but it's the dream I am
writing after not before, and my waking has developed
into a long aisle of disappointment as I begin to type: "a
sunbeam shines through the window pane, illuminating
the otherwise invisible dust, so I blow in the beam's
direction and examine the illuminated flecks of dust as
they overturn and swirl: 'The cognition of an external
object already presupposes the distinction of outside
and inside, subject and object, the perceiving and the
perceived / When this separation takes place, and is
recognized as such, and clung to, the primary nature of
the experience is forgotten, and from this an endless
series of entanglements, intellectual and emotional,
takes its rise,' recalling the moment of sitting with Andy

on the lake, 'what is ordering the images' attachments to each other and what is causing some of them to brighten enough to stand out against the shifting background of their origin,' I sit up on the couch, wave my hand through the sunbeam, and watch a reworking of the past as the dust continues to swirl forward despite my having stopped the waving movement of my hand" — "this evening I looked through all of Brad's printed photographs, and among the stacks of 4x6 photos arranged neatly in cigar boxes I found one Brad took of me sitting on the beach on the tip of a peninsula steadying my camera in the direction of a ring-billed gull, and I felt startled by the photo as I held it in my hands because I had forgotten that moment from twenty years before, or forgotten to remember it, and I suddenly recalled in detail the feeling of Brad standing in the sand several feet away, barefoot, holding up his old Pentax, while I, holding my own camera, pulled back on the film advance lever with my thumb and released the shutter for that blinked instant, to retrieve forever the relation of the gull to the shoreline; a strange feeling now, wondering how a photo of me taken by Brad would predict such a powerful relation to him in my mind, that the photo of me was not only a memory of Brad, but also a bridge into his breathing self, aged sixteen, and the record of my own action is in fact an embodiment of Brad, standing in friendship on the beach with the full sweep of his life before him" . . .

. . . I remember when I thought Robert Grenier was the most famous person in the whole world, Lewis says, lightening the mood, then I show him *Index Cards* and explain the way I stumbled upon it that morning while I was looking for a text to link me back to summer, and also how I came to find it through an algorithm when I was searching for a different book concerned with elliptical thinking: "More important to me than fidelity and adherence to a medium is a kind of devotion to promiscuity / an embrace of materials, formats, histories and genres, and lastly but perhaps most importantly, an investment in language / I am a believer in heterogeneity as an enabler and enhancer of the story wanting to be told," where writing opens up as a process of recognizing the language that already surrounds us, more of a power of attunement than a power of creation, but how does one teach that, Chuck asked, how does one teach that to a group of students within the cellar walls of the classroom; he was preparing to teach a course the following day on C. D. Wright's beech trees, yet our conversation began with his description of the morning's peregrination with Cathy, they found the screech owl but not the Oregon junco, so they would need to go back to look more carefully again — are we in the middle of one of your poems, Zoë asks, as Benjamin breaks the challah and passes it around the table, the question arising from my description of a feeling upon waking in the afternoon from a nap, in which memory was not a narrative structure but rather a vast heap of experience tangled together in the most

inextricable form, where only edges were visible and I
had to climb upon the heap of my memory in order to
extract even the smallest fragment, this being my
description of the feeling of waking and not of the
dream, my thinking now about the light in Murnane's
study passing through his kaleidoscope: "When I first
held my kaleidoscope up to my left eye and turned my
face towards the window, certain rays of the same
sunlight that passed through that glass marble and then
through the metal tube towards my eye would have
travelled past my face and then across the room and
would then have reached the book mentioned / Today,
however, while I write these words, I am unable to
recall, let alone to report, what I saw while I looked
down the tube and through the glass marble and into
the afternoon sunlight," in the same way I am not able to
recall what I was thinking about when Owen, aged four,
held his translucent toy tile up to the bright morning
window as I watched from across the room, the bril-
liancy of the sunshine set the magenta tile alight, casting
its color onto the yellow wall opposite the window,
perhaps I was thinking about the difference between
natural and artificial light, how one illuminates the
entire world while the other provides a small patch of
legibility: "Owen and I arrange magnetic toy tiles on the
light table, triangles with triangles, squares with squares,
the tiles are translucent and emit beautiful tones of
magenta, sea green, cerulean and sun yellow, and when
we arrange the tallest triangles into an octagon we turn it
in circles, then rearrange the pieces into a new order,
and repeat until Owen takes one tile over to the window
and holds it up to the daylight, 'a castle made of walls

that retain light instead of scattering it beyond the
perimeter of our being, with several turrets on the
outside edges to keep watch over our miniature
kingdom,' the blue of the castle wall matches Owen's
shirt, which I point out, but when he takes the tile off
the light table and places it next to his shirt, its brilliance
is lost without being backlit, so I prop him up on the
table such that both the cloth of his shirt and the tile are
illuminated, it's true, he says, stretching out the fabric of
his shirt on the table, they're the same, the colors, and
this seems to satisfy him, because it correlates some-
thing about his own life to the world at large" — "there
is a sadness that rests calmly at the end of the word,
there are cardinals singing in the pines, also, there is a
meter I would like to find that would displace separation
and soothe silence at the end of the word, a rotation of
pages beyond the spine, a scattering in the air of singing
pages, what would it mean to pick up the sadness at the
end of the word and place it neatly below the text, so it
aligns properly the pine boughs with sunshine," this
being my attempt to respond to the line in Brossard's
poem, "We will have to agree over what inside us says it
is suffering," which seems like an increasingly difficult
task, but if we cannot find consensus on suffering it feels
like we are doomed, "we will have to agree over the
color of artillery shells so we do not confuse them with
the pure beauty of sea and sky," are we in the middle of
the poem yet, I'm wondering, as I stand up to water the
houseplant whose tag reads, "Hello, my friends call me
Gold Crest False Aralia, I enjoy medium light," hello
Aralia, I say, as I water it over the sink, the weight of the
potting soil steadily increases before water drips through

the drain holes below the flax-flower blue of the stained
glass plate hanging in the window above the sink:
"When one colour approaches slightly to another, it is
said to incline towards it; when it stands in the middle
between two colours, it is said to be intermediate; when,
on the contrary, it evidently approaches very near to one
of the colours, it is said to fall, or pass into it," in which
ultramarine blue is compared to the upper side of the
wings of a small blue heath butterfly, and flax-flower
blue is compared to the light parts of the margin of the
wings of devil's butterfly, there being no way to measure
the experience of color, therefore descriptions of color
are always dependent upon comparison and their
relation to other colors, similar to language in many
respects, and perhaps also suffering — why are you
lying on the ground, Papa, Liza asks as she crouches
down beside the trail to see what I see from the ground,
it's the best way to photograph the twinflower, I reply, as
I push lightly on a slender stem, which causes the paired,
small, pale pink flowers to nod above their evergreen
leaves, and Liza does the same to another stem causing
that flowerhead to nod as the other comes back to a
partial rest, then we take our hands and lightly brush
across a whole group of twinflowers, and there are
hundreds of flowerheads before us, growing discreetly
in a "colonial mat," as the field guide informs us, and the
word colonial lingers as I read further to discover the
twinflower is actually a dwarf shrub in the honeysuckle
family, which makes sense, given its luxuriance, *Linnaea
borealis*, Linnaeus's favorite flower, and as we hike
further toward the meadow then down to the creek in
search of elephant's head flower, Liza points out an

awkwardly grown spruce tree and asks if it's a marker
tree; I browse the field guide again and recall the
common name that describes the family in which the
elephant's head flower resides, that it attaches itself to
the root structure of neighboring plants through
haustoria, slender parasitic structures extending out and
piercing the roots of a host plant to absorb nutrients,
and the word haustoria reminds me of hysteria, its own
roots a pejorative description of a frenzy that was
thought to be peculiar to women by its association with
a supposed floating womb that would move about the
body, these thoughts pass as a Steller's jay scolds the
valley with its guttural call while Liza and Owen take
turns walking the balance beam of a log that once
supported a cabin wall — the dream itself was staged in
a reading room in Memorial Library in Madison, where
everything I had ever written was placed on long tables,
and people I didn't recognize were wandering between
the tables, stopping now and again to pick up an item
they examined from several angles but did not, as far as I
could tell, actually read any of the language printed on
the pages, and in the far corner by the north-facing
windows sat Andy, who wore a bow tie and a bowler's
hat, eating from a container of serviceberries he had just
gathered from the trees whose limbs were visible if one
approached the windows and looked down to the street
below, and as I approached him he started speaking, but
I couldn't understand a word he was saying because it
sounded very much like a pretend language he would, in
waking life, make up as a kind of art to accompany one
of his songs, and when I asked him what he meant, he
offered me some serviceberries, then he pointed to a

sheet at the edge of the closest table on which was printed an etymology: "The name serviceberry has its own folklore dating back to pioneer days when the showy flowering, marking the end of winter, coincided with memorial services for people who died during the winter season; according to others, services were deferred until the blooming signaled the time when the soil could be turned and the bodies buried in the ground"...

3-25-22   Madison, WI

... I wake in the poets' house from a dream softened by
my knowledge of having fallen asleep here several hours
earlier, realizing then in the darkness that perhaps the
dreams of the poets were stored in the floorboards and
walls in such a way that my own dreams could speak to
them or trace the memory of their manifestation, and
this thought guided me back into a deep sleep such that
in waking now I remember the soft comfort it afforded
me, the symmetry between waking then and now, and
the dream between those waking moments that was
in itself a kind of awakening has left me feeling rested
as though I had completed a poem that was accessible
only to my dreaming self and which had prepared
me to awaken and begin a different poem here in the
morning — Rick mentions an essay he read about
difference and similarity, how a subject can be expressed
in detail through either one, and I agree with the author,
I say, because when identifying species in the field one
uses both similarity and difference to narrow down
the species among others with traits either similar or
different, that you need both in order to really know a
thing, then I read an entry about the northern shrike
that Chuck sent in reply to my text that read, "northern
shrike," along with a picture of the marsh but not the
shrike: "since they lack talons, they stun or kill their prey
with blows from their powerful beaks, then, if they do
not eat their prey immediately, they impale it on thorns
or barbed wire," I open *Mushroom Book* to show Rick
the reproductions of lithographic mushroom prints and
the semi-transparent sheets that cover them, each print

folded into quarters, such that when it is unfolded the transparent sheet sits on top of the image, and on each transparent sheet is printed a series of textual objects including a field guide description of the mushroom represented as well as quotes from philosophical and religious texts, mushroom poems, mushroom narratives, even excerpts from Thoreau's *Journal*: "Last year, the / last three weeks of / August, the woods were / filled with the strong / musty scent of decaying fungi, / but this year I have seen very / few fungi, and have not noticed that / odor at all – a failure more perceptible / to the frogs and toads," a reader must confront the text before absorbing the image below to negotiate their harmonies, a veil before the image's ultimate sharpness — the biting wind off the lake causes Rick and me to throw up our hoods against the onslaught as we wonder aloud whether it is starting to rain or if the wind is picking up water from the river and pelting it against our faces, and as we look out at the empty water I recount my writing from earlier in the morning: "thousands of ducks and other divers on the north end of Lake Waubesa yesterday evening: buffleheads, ring-necked ducks, scaups, hooded mergansers, gadwalls, common loons, shovelers, coots, goldeneyes, among many others, I had to carry several handkerchiefs to dry the lenses of my binoculars that kept being blurred by the freezing rain, eventually the handkerchiefs grew too wet and merely spread the water around the lenses, which caused the figures of the birds to appear mottled and indistinguishable; I began to walk back and stop my collection of species names as the birds on the lake became hundreds of small figures whose colors and particularities were lost in the rain, my position on the shoreline relative to their distance made inaccessible by the near-freezing waters of the lake, its eastern margin consisted of a wreck of ice sheets pounded on top of one another by the sheer force of the storms, then I returned to the contours of the path, listening to the rain whipped by wind until a particular bend in the trail stopped my movement as a memory of Owen, aged two, while he ran around the same bend in the trail during the month of May ten years before, began to combine with the feelings of nostalgia and wanderlust that had brought me here despite a host of obligations in Iowa, and I understood that seeking an emotion is much different than seeking the company of a loved one, that I was standing in the freezing rain accompanied by myself alone, the memory of Owen warmed me but not enough to produce the presence I had come here to reproduce even though I knew that form of reproduction is impossible," that it's some form of self-deception, Rick says, as we round the hill to look out across the marsh, there's a curious insistence in the way we return to writing despite knowing its instability, its overall failure at transcribing experience, but at least we desire it, as if the possibility of the accuracy of language suggests that living could be like writing, which is a kind of mortal opening in the face of an indeterminacy that we have come to rely on in order to continue, and as we make our way down the boardwalk to a small pond that is almost perfectly circular, I recall to Rick the time he sent me a picture of his poem that he wrote here with a stick in the pondweed that simply read "pondweed"...

. . ."when I look back through a thicket of time I grow
satisfied not by the plain texture of my life's story, not
by the secure structure of its becoming, but by the
sheer unreliability of its patterning, as if my self divides
but I remain unaware of its division until I return to
my starting point," the writing near the end of the start
of this same composition one year ago, the sentence
becoming a yearlong sentence that is about to loop back
onto itself through the imagination of its traceability: "I
desire completely to be transported inside the text, to
take up residence there, the way one may for a long time
stare into a photograph and actuate the contours of its
prior reality that somehow brushes against the present
with such startling intensity the interval evaporates
beyond the serviceberry flowering on the hillside above
me," bloodroot and spring beauties blossoming below
the kinglets, the minor whitewater sound of the river as
it runs across a wide scattering of stones, the memory
of the writing "fading and growing with intensity as the
clouds come and go and I find my footing upon the
trail, where there is nothing profound, where there is
no profundity in the long-beaked sedge, only this song
of visibility to carry further into the day as I remember
the various forms of assignment I have given myself to
justify the splendid non-being of my mind in relation
to the ironwoods" — "The corona has shrunk to twice
the size / of the moon and there is nothing left to / type
from the notebook as I take off my / reading glasses to
watch two milkweed / seeds unfolded from the bundle
of seeds / in an open milkweed pod but still / attached

lift and fall in the breeze, the / text blurring every time I
turn my eyes / back to the screen and the seed inside the
/ looser pod // inside the looser pod becoming, to my
/ accustomed eyes, sharper and more central // Jordan
said in the space of reading / *Austerlitz* he couldn't
sleep and was trying / to give up the notion of the loss
of place / when at nine he moved from Marquette / to
Antioch, a coincidence of time and / place that joined
the day to a particular / landscape and left it lost in the
new one / Also Owen is eight soon nine and they /
might move also, revisiting the / coincident loss on the
child," "which patterned for me the mimicry of desire,
that is, the desire to go outside and become a thing in
a world despite already being a being in the world, the
desire to be more than oneself through the observation
of the outer world and its way of becoming internalized
through this music we bring forward to the moment
of composition" — "it is good that a year still feels
like a long time, my sense of who I am now not being
entirely coincident with who I was then, a promise for
the possibility of change that I am no longer recogniz-
able to myself in the present moment looking back at
myself in a previous time," this thought inscribed onto
the page causes me to pause, stand up, and approach the
bedroom window where I look down onto the garden
that I was writing about only a few minutes ago, it being
summer in the poem's garden but not in the world: "I
fetch a field knife to harvest arugula and beet greens,
and as I kneel down to cut the tallest plants in the row
I notice how clean and fresh the leaves are from yester-
day's rain, the leaves had lain down upon the straw after
the shower only to rise up again in the morning's sun

that now streams through the kitchen window as I open
the patio door and step inside, fill up a canning jar with
water to hold tall stems of spearmint that will keep well
in the ambient air for several days or more," although,
the season is quickly shifting as the snowfall melts and
the Carolina wren mixes its caroling with the high song
of the chickadee, soon vultures will arrive tipping their
long wings to soar high on thermals above the river
valley, snow trillium will part the browned leaves on
the forest floor, nettles will appear beside the creek,
the season will shift fully and this moment will be its
own retrospect along the cascading overfills of beauty
and its interlays of grief — "But most musicians can't
hear a single sound, they listen only to the relationship
between two or more sounds / Music for them has
nothing to do with their powers of audition, but only to
do with their powers of observing relationships," there's
a gap in the classroom discourse that allows the outside
world to start trickling in as I walk to the window that
overlooks the canopy of several oaks, and after a long
period of silence I offer the question, what is the author
trying to say here, which is met by more silence until
finally a student at the back of the classroom answers
that there's a difference between listening and doing —
is that a little strong, I'm wondering, "interlays of grief," I
can't really concentrate any longer, I am tired, that's all I
know, and everyone else is tired, yet the poem continues
and I open Vogel's book to read: "we come to language /
as architects of relation – // but sentences are not secure
// we take them up as planks / and make unstable
geometries // a book arrives in threads – " it being a
book about bird nests and also the way language and

memory combine to form nests, interweaving hundreds
of strands of various materials, sometimes human-made
materials like newspaper or book scraps where words
are printed, or leftover linen thread that would bind a
book together, the question of whether the robins in my
backyard would build a nest out of thin strips of poems,
reminding me of Lisa's poem: "Now when I brush
my hair I take the hair out of the brush and instead of
putting it in the compost container on the sink, I put it
outside in the grass for birds to find and use" — while
I was writing the previous lines, I originally removed
the quotation marks around the writing from April
15, 2021, and considered whether or not those lines
maintained a fluidity that was desirable only a few
moments ago as I read those lines without their borders
into the air of the room where I now find myself, then
I again inserted the quotation marks around last year's
writing, it having been, for a brief period, this moment's
writing, before deleting the following passage: "being
only myself, it appears, that I can inscribe upon the page
despite the distances I create between myself and the
text, it is obvious in this sounding-out that I become
nothing more than words, and I've decided that this
is problematic and slightly off-key following the line,
'through this music we bring forward to the moment
of composition,' but now I find myself quite uncertain
about both of those choices as the wind gusts and
the red buds of the red maple bend forward in their
reddening, 'as I crouch to examine the large-flowered
bellwort rising from a wreath of trout lily and hepatica
leaves, its yellow flowers drooping at the end of thin
stems, and as I lean further to see if I can view the

inside of a flower without propping it up, my ear nearly touches the ground as my cheek brushes the ephemeral leaves from which the bellwort rises'"...

... "I trim yellow lilies and place them in a vase on the
porch table where I've also poured water into a bowl
containing small stones collected from Lake Superior
last summer, and because we found them in quiet,
shallow water it occurred to me this is their most recent
and likely preferred environment, so I should give
them a soak every evening as though I were watering
the lilies that preside gently above them; the fireflies
begin lighting up in the garden glowing among the pale
purple coneflowers, spikenard, a row of echinacea, and
the bats have begun feeding in the open air between
darkening limbs of walnuts, I see them by their contrast
to the fading light in spaces between branches, their
disappearance beyond the canopy relative to my point
of observation but not to the night which sustains
them" — I brace the kayak and slide my legs inside the
hull, then begin paddling through the evening light that
plays colors upon the undulations of the minor waves
where the river's current enters the lake, and as I pass
into the lake from the river and leave one threshold
behind while the nighthawks call in the open sky, I
remember one year ago I arrived in Portland hoping
that the "elsewheres would converge," as Calvino puts
it, "this reconstruction of the world accomplished in the
absence of the world," the loss of a friend who I conjured
by accessing the landscape of memory, I found myself
not writing the past but a list of vegetables in the garden,
or describing the tidal patterns in the sand I walked
across for hours after encountering a pair of marbled
godwits probing the shoreline, these hesitancies made

necessary by the complete expanse of the ocean, my
diminutive human scale before the waves that exploded
upon outlying sea stacks, or the height of the trail along
the Clackamas River, most people die before reaching
the bottom, they get wrapped around a tree, Brad said,
as we hiked past a cliff drop on our way to the waterfall,
several hundred feet to the whitewater below — the
rope ladder up to the tree house swings toward the
trunk as Liza scrambles up and pulls herself through
the opening in the floor, she peers back down toward
me and says, come on it's easy, as my adult center of
gravity swings my body fast toward the trunk I nearly
fall backward until I reach toward the highest rung on
the ladder and pull myself up by my arms, using my feet
for balance alone: "Again I am attracted by the deep
scarlet of the wild moss rose, half open in the grass,
all glowing with rosy light," "Why is this flower saying
the same thing over and over like it doesn't believe I'm
listening," Liza laughs as I struggle toward the top of the
ladder and finally emerge onto the treehouse platform,
she walks to the edge and sits down to show me how we
can dangle our feet over the side, the breeze comes up
from the river and cools our legs and bare feet but not
our upper bodies because the wind is blocked by the
trunk of the spruce, it's kind of like dipping your feet in
water, she says — of places to begin the poem, all places
are available, this is to say, all places are available for
beginning, not just in the poem but elsewhere, and this
feels important when considering the sunlight illumi-
nating the green and yellow curtain upon which the lilac
is silhouetted in the early evening light; I glance up from
Gladman's book as a bird lands in silhouette upon the

lilac, its song, the cardinal's song, fills the room where
I sit and wait for the next association to describe its
own wandering path in relation to its original impulse,
as if there's a perfect way to be lost through one's not
wondering whether being lost exists in the negative
sphere: "These places will let evening glow through
them and outline thresholds of ascendent and descen-
dent thinking," "These paragraphs will be the boundary
between wind and ground and will be woven into the
thing that is writing; they will be a feeling of the thing
in motion but will hang invisibly to void" — a kingbird
perches on the shoreline willow extending its branch
horizontally above the water, the bark is worn down
smooth from years of children walking out on the trunk
to peer down into the shallows, to leap into the swirls
of minnows who nibble at one's ankles while wading in
the water, the bluegill, perhaps, or the pumpkinseed, it
occurs to me this lake is just like any other in this part of
the Midwest, but my attachment to its particular satu-
ration is defined by repetition, therefore its shoreline is
a distinct parameter holding evidence of my being, and
its mirroring of the past soothes the anxiety embedded
within me, "Writing is not linked to knowing, but to
being / Writing is the home of being," being the reso-
nance of my interior echoes before the deepening blue
of the eastern sky, and as I turn the kayak back toward
the river's mouth I find that the bats have come out
to join the nighthawks: "I remember a moment some
years ago when I captured a bat who was loose in our
apartment, it took up a position on the ceiling in such
a way that I could trap it by setting a plastic container
around its frightened body, then I moved a lid along the

55

ceiling and carefully guided the bat into the container before I carried the poor creature outside; as I walked down the steps into the backyard I couldn't feel its presence, its lightness made me wonder if it had somehow escaped, but as I held the container away from my body and unfastened the lid, the bat flew off rapidly and disappeared into the trees, and I remember wondering if I felt it fly from the container, or if the movement of unfastening the lid combined with the bat's tiny propulsion to erase any evidence of its departure, how in handling the bat this way I experienced the movement of its flight, seemingly erratic but in perfect harmony with its purpose" . . .

. . . "so that instead of drifting into sleep I slid into my memories / Or rather, the memories (at least so it seemed to me) rose higher and higher in some space outside of myself, until, having reached a certain level, they overflowed from that space into me, like water over the top of a weir," I close my eyes and sit up in bed, my failure to desire desiring at this juncture as the wind picks up and its background hush mimics this slow unfolding while I count breaths, attempt to dissipate the sleeplessness before me, as if the thought that brushes against the moment could pass by in its near weightlessness and be replaced by another instead of embedding itself sharply so as to cause a miniature throbbing that the meditated breath merely accentuates in the small gap between the inhale and the exhale, there is your mind at work again, I remind myself, like the infinite arc of omniscience that fails to dissolve its own self-recognition: "But awaiting – just as it is not related to the future any more than to an accessible past – is also the awaiting of awaiting, which does not situate us in a present, for 'I' have always already awaited what I will always wait for: the immemorable, the unknown which has no present, and which I can no more remember than I can know whether I am not forgetting the future" — I walk down the narrow forest path bordered by violets and archangel to reach the less crowded forest floor, where I pinch off a single flower from the wild leeks whose umbels nod among trilliums in the afternoon light, and as the rich garlicky scent rises from the flower and disperses into the morning air, I carry it with me on my fingertips

further down the trail where the word 'allium' stirs a
memory, for a reason I cannot properly define, of one
afternoon when I sat with Lisa on her front porch before
her manuscript and a bowl of Concord grapes, when
she explained to me that she didn't want the project I
was printing for her to be presented loose-leaf because
there was a power, perhaps even a somewhat mystical
power, if I remember her explanation correctly, that
is exercised when paper is bound together in a book
form, and I related what she was saying, in part, to the
power of folding paper, that once a sheet is folded into
a new shape it is forever something different than what
it was originally, its essence is changed even though the
trace of its origin remains the same; the trail opens into
a cherry orchard where the sight of the ripe red fruits
hanging from the boughs causes me to walk further
until I discover a wooden rowboat at the back of the
orchard surrounded by fallow grasses, its hull partially
decomposed, covered by moss interspersed with small
brackens and knapweeds, and as I approach the disin-
tegrating boat I notice the oar locks are not rusted, they
are still attached to the gunwales, so I test the strength
of the oars and find they are strangely solid, set into the
locks as though the boat had been prepared presently
for the water despite being abandoned several decades
ago at the edge of an orchard miles from the nearest
lake — "I seem to need some concept of accelerating
ignorance, an increasing quantity measuring per day the
connections not made and implications not drawn by
me," the intersection is not manufactured but is simply
the point of consequence one comes to in the course of
a day, or the course of a lifetime, and it's true that I've

been wondering about free will and my own ability to measure the distance between the action I feel like I desire and the action I end up receiving, so to speak, as if it comes from somewhere beyond myself and I am merely its agent, and perhaps this is part of the reason I keep writing through the writing of others, not because their texts possess a determination in my selection of them, but because of the randomness with which they manifest in my life: "Thank you for your letter, I began a composition this morning from the transcription of your transcription, which is still in process, and attached here inside the process of its becoming" — Jack says he is still planning to go to Oregon after he plays a gig in Grand Junction if the head gasket on his truck will make it that far, the next stop being Mariko's place in Eugene before moving up to Portland, it's hard to know if the reception by our friends will match the excitement I have for this trip, he says, because my life's momentum is directed toward this period of wandering and comparable freedom, while everyone else is caught in the middle of various domestic routines, and in reply to Jack's thoughts I can only offer a gesture of silence while I consider the balance of risks that has led me to my own senses of responsibility, "Hope, which is, after all, no more than a splint of thought / Projected outward," so I'm wondering if travel is for Jack, as it is for me, a form of delay as well as a perpetual becoming, having known each other for this long it seems probable that we'll stay mostly the same for another twenty years despite the fact that all possible actions can be met with all possible outcomes at any moment in time, "It's not that miracles are achieved, nor that we / make them happen as we

sweep away all the / remnants of that other life we keep
thinking is / the best one to possess," I read aloud to
Jack after we are done talking, as I promised, not to read
to him in the present state of our now former conversa-
tion but in its afterglow, as one might send a spirit aloft
as a gesture of goodwill even if one questions the reality
of the spirit that is sent aloft . . .

7-23-22   *Ames, IA*

. . . as the daytime heat dissipates from 105 to 95
degrees, I walk out the door into early evening and
make my way slowly down the narrow paths bordering
the creek, where I try to determine if the scene before
me is beautiful or if it has simply been made beautiful
by repetition: "the evening sunlight vaulted from the
horizon's clouds in long rays collected by a thinner
line of clouds above me, such that the far clouds were
backlit with their edges glowing in the setting sun, and
the clouds over my head were underlit by breakthrough
rays emitted through various gaps in the cloudbank that
rested upon the horizon," you haven't been reading,
I think aloud as I pass the faded sign that reads "Bike
Path Open" to look out across the recently mown hay
field, I notice some of the birds are not singing who
normally sing here when the grass is high, yet the deer
path winding down to the woods is still visible between
the collection lines of drying hay, a curving indenta-
tion my eye follows to the shrub line above the creek;
I am always reading something whether I mean to or
not, there are infinite books here in the contours of
the landscape, and perhaps the wildness I'm searching
for is the same kind of record regardless of where it is
sourced — "I crest the rise that reveals Greenwood
Park and make my way to the small prairie restoration
above the artificial pond, its open grown oak recalls
Wisconsin, the particulars of the Iowan landscape
uncanny as I understand them while a red-winged
blackbird calls from the patch of planted cattails and
I am struck by the deepest sense of loss since arriving

here in August, and my amazement by the strength
of that emotion is enough to cure me of it as I run my
hand through the bluestem culms and direct my body
back toward the empty apartment," I no longer need to
feel the same sense of failure at those seams where one
joins the past with the future, which is not quite the
present but something more like an adequate presence,
as getting up now to pour more coffee I notice the
cicadas have not started calling and only the distant
running of the wren's song sustains the morning's air;
what does it mean to carry a cycle around in one's
mind, remembering the repetition three years ago of
walking along the creek in Des Moines and falling into
the same depressive logic, inside of which I was wholly
to blame for my family's placement in what felt like a
trap but which now, in leaving, feels like a test of will
that I managed to complete in some satisfactory way,
the writing of presence without a destination or plan of
any kind, the small notes that accumulate into a block of
language without a purposeful arrangement, like a proof
text for living, the day's tasks could result in packing
the entire house or simply lounging on this porch in
order to re-filter the past through several new frames
of narrative, this idea of discovery through the act of
composition seems to rely on the fiction of removing
oneself completely, or focusing first on the rich green
color of the hickory leaves in the morning sun, then
the memory of the butterflies, the hackberry emperors
and red admirals who rested on the window screen as I
transcribed several passages from the novels held open
with beach stones: "It is a fundamentally insane notion
that one is able to influence the course of events by a

turn of the helm, by willpower alone, whereas in fact all
is determined by the most complex interdependencies,"
"And when I looked down from this vantage point I
saw the labyrinth, the light sandy ground, the sharply
delineated contours of hedges taller than a man and
almost pitch-black now – a pattern simple in compar-
ison with the tortuous trail I had behind me, but one
which I knew in my dream, with absolute certainty,
represented a cross-section of my brain," "The disquiet
I experienced because of that momentary failure to see
what was meant – I now sometimes feel that at that
moment I beheld an image of death – lasted only a very
short time, and passed over me like the shadow of a
bird in flight"— Liza appears from behind the garage
and walks over to ask what I'm up to, I'm writing about
the morning, I say, now you're in the poem, too, and as
she approaches me I see she is carrying a small basket
of cherries that we picked yesterday in the afternoon
heat, placed in mesh bags and dunked in barrels of cold
water before we brought them home, so now we each
eat a few and take turns seeing how far we can spit the
pits into the garden before she says, OK Papa, you can
finish your writing now; as she wanders down a short
trail away from me I'm left with the taste of cherries
and the image of clouds parting in a shift to sunlight
that rays down through the aspen leaves, I watch leaf
shadow emit scintillations of light between the leaflets
and consider the relationship between the weir and
the waterfall I contemplated earlier in the month, that
the overwhelming force is not those memories which,
as it were, fall down upon me from a great height due
to a gravity I cannot control, but the sheer volume of

other memories pushing those forward, the countless
tributaries I cannot see or name but which nonetheless
fill the reservoir that continually overflows without
my knowledge as to why, at any given moment, I may
shudder once again before a recollection of great shame,
or turn instead to the budding hickory on the slope
above Walnut Creek in mid-spring, whose leaves unfurl
from a warm orange covering that resembles the petals
of flowers, and whose neighbors, the buckeyes, have a
genus name, *Aesculus*, that closely resembles Aeschylus
— "I am an action that starts or stops whose pain isn't
real and who grafts absence onto an unrecoverable
past, the primrose is also an action, the wild senna too,
endlessness enchants the seeker between one's own
action and another, what it means to be certain is less
interesting than what it means to be uncertain, though
I'm forever lost between them in my willingness to
replay the past: 'the first night camping alone miles from
other people I was terrified by the thought of death
patrolling around me, and last summer it returned when
I was camping alone and I heard a faint buzzing hum in
the darkness that I could not locate as being from within
or without, and walking through the woods by the light
of my headlamp, searching for the source of the noise,
I finally understood it was from within and therefore
unable to be accounted for,' there are always several
senses in motion before their combinatory impact can
be felt or understood, which recalls the feeling I worked
through in the weeks after Brad died when I felt largely
like an imposter, as if my grief were invented and did not
truly scale to the friendship as he would have perceived
it before he died: 'The now familiar backdrop of maples

and beeches among the morning songs of wood pewees and hermit thrushes, the way I write those names again and feel some affect about the near past looping back into the present like an ambient recording on repeat, the songs' undulations wash lightly against a private time that never collapses but simply dissolves into another frame of reference,'" the same song from the thrush eight years ago in the Saint Regis Canoe Area as I assembled my tent at a small island campsite, where the song's ethereal sweetness seemed to disappear by infinitesimal degrees until it vanished completely, my ear still recognized an afterthought as if the song could only dissipate by percolating through my memory, its register in the world being different than its register in my mind . . .

. . . "Here in the forest am I here the second / and third
fourth and fifth of Jordan's / bird songs had mourning in
them for / Jordan because he had lived to deliver them
in that way they were delivered," because I had lived to
deliver them in that way they were delivered, Rick's
notes from 9-23-18 while he sat, as he later told me,
obscured by the vegetation off the side of a trail in Forest
Park, where he could hear the conversations of the
passing joggers, "I've always been wanting not any
drama / a woman jogging past with three dogs says / to
the other," his reflection on the previous day's trip to the
river gorge composed in his notes that I later found again
in his manuscript, a section titled 'This Present Tense:'
"Brad turned a tottering circle clutching the dog,
Trapper, to his chest on slippery slanted moss cliff path
50 feet above the rocks and water he didn't worry or fall
he scrambled up to the proper path / Jordan turned
around and crossed again the gap that made him feel
death close / Later I heard mourning in the bird songs
he performed," and my memory of testing rock holds as
I crossed again the gap, several of the rocks loosened and
crashed down into the river canyon before a secure
outcrop and an overhanging root were enough to bring
me back to the other side, to "this present tense that
refuses no one," and only several minutes later Brad,
Rick, and I found the proper path that led to the hot
springs beside the river, where we drank beers as if
nothing had happened, where mist hovered above the
spring and obscured our view of the canyon and its dark
overreaching evergreens as I recounted the situation on

the cliff and the cold sweat that I discovered soaking my
entire body after I crossed back over to the other side, it
was clear that our proximity to death is much closer than
we imagine, that we are living inside its parameters even
as we disregard its own present tense, that this present
tense that refuses no one, is, in fact, death, how fear
encircled my body as I undressed and tested the
temperature of the water, how as I eased myself down
into the rock pool the adrenaline that brought me to that
point must have been, at some level, mixed with the mist
that was rising before my eyes, covering my body, and
fogging my view of the very cliff from which I had
almost slipped to my death, which affected, I imagine,
my performance of the Nashville warbler's song as I
stood before an audience at David's bookstore, or, at
least, Rick's perception of those songs: "wee-see-wee-see
wit-a-wit-a-wit, wee-see-wee-see wit-a-wit-a-wit," a hint
of sulfur from the hot spring still clung to my hair as I
combed it with my fingers before the audience as a way
to stay embodied while waiting ten seconds before the
next song, "wee-see-wee-see wit-a-wit-a-wit, wee-see-
wee-see wit-a-wit-a-wit" — I stake New England asters
that are leaning over nearly to the ground, a green stake
on either side and then several lengths of garden twine
strung back and forth to give the high stems a place to
rest, the flowers now positioned upright toward the
sunlight, permitting passage to the vegetable beds where
I gather beet greens, oregano and chives, then return to
the kitchen; a text arrives while I rinse the beet greens, it
is Steve, I think, who said he would forward the
complaints from the circuit court filed by Brad's estate,
so I sit down on the kitchen floor to scroll through each

page of the lawsuit, section 44 reads: "The negligence and/or fault of defendants, and each of them, in one or more of the particulars set forth herein, was a substantial factor in causing, contributing to, and/or enhancing the following injuries, and ultimately the death of plaintiff's decedent: Blunt head trauma; Numerous fractures of the head and face; Multiple skull fractures; Multiple maxilla and mandible fractures; Numerous lacerations, contusions, and abrasions of the head and face," remembering now that after Nicky returned from the funeral home she carried the clothes she had chosen for Brad and placed them on the counter, then she took me aside and explained that the director had advised against even a private viewing; recognizability, I'm thinking, as I chop the chives and strip the oregano and add them to the cast-iron pan where the beet greens are sautéing, as the kitchen fills with the scent of the herbs, as I stir them in the pan and then fold them into the greens, as several measures of memory are compared in the reactivation of a single moment in time and the precision of the language in establishing blame: "The Genie S-85 incident Boom Lift, which was designed, manufactured, tested, inspected, and distributed by defendants Terex and Genie, and was leased and/or rented by defendant Herc to defendant Pickathon and/or the GuildWorks defendants in the summer of 2019, continued to tip approximately another One-Hundred-Ten degrees (110°) with both Swet and Blackmore on the platform until it impacted the ground; both Swet and Blackmore suffered traumatic brain injuries and were both declared deceased at the site by the medical examiner," the echo of Luke's text on the day of the accident, "call me as soon

as you see this," like a pinch in the arm as I set pasta to boil and remove the cast-iron pan from the flame — a rainbow is an angle of observation, I reply to Liza who asks if I can see the rainbow that she sees as I water the new-seeded grass, then I hand her the hose so I can see from where she saw the rainbow in the angled morning sun, and what the sentence means is a notation for preceding events, either reading or walking or listening to the walking in the reading; I take the smallest beach stone collected from Oregon and place it on the S key of my laptop, then the T, the O, the N, & the E, but I do not enter into the moment of writing by applying pressure to the stone, rather, the stone simply rests on a single key before I move it to another, it is a kind of spelling of s-t-o-n-e so the machine feels something more like itself, something less anxious than human, now the emptiness of the room with the books closed as I write: "Rick mentioned his friend, a visual artist, who would always make studies before a major work, and it never occurred to Rick that a writer could do that too, and how he was most attracted to his friend's studies for larger works, not the works themselves; my describing to Laura yesterday that I no longer want to write but simply to walk and have my body record a line of text that doesn't resemble writing but resembles the feeling of reading when printed, like an infinite spectrogram that performs a binding in its wake, therefore I do not even need to print it because it will print itself and bind itself and appear in chronological order on the bookshelf, and the collection of these walks will be my life's work, not even notes for the larger work, but a larger work composed of notes"
— I turn to reading old journals and find notes on the

walk I took with Rick in the middle of October 2018, when Rick mentioned his friend, the visual artist, as we walked past ninebark shrubs and goldenrods at the marsh, his having given me a printout of transcribed poem notes from 9-23-18 about his time sitting in Forest Park in Portland shortly after we read together at David's, where we alternated our readings back and forth so no one took precedence, my wondering again what it was about the bird song performed from the human voice that revealed mourning, or perhaps it was the silent interval between songs that revealed mourning, my having stopped for ten seconds between each song, creating a long gap in the sense of vocal embodiment for the audience that included Brad, a mourning in the void of performative action, Rick and I passing the ninebark and my asking if we could pause so I could take pictures of the autumn leaves and then of the branches, turning to my journals tonight not to harvest some remarkable passage but to configure the repetition of my grief, then finding a passage written after that very same walk in October, "Rick dropped me at a cafe next to Batch Bakehouse, I had a croissant, a coffee, read *Landforms of Iowa*, then walked to Atwood to meet Laura," how unremarkable are the private passings of time and the ego tightened neatly into its folding, hundreds of unmarked pages in Brad's copy of *Remembrance of Things Past* finally arrive at the underlined passage: "And it is, after all, as good a way as any of solving the problem of existence to get near enough to the things and people that have appeared to us beautiful and mysterious from a distance to be able to satisfy ourselves that they have neither mystery nor beauty"...

Notes

This book employs many intertexts and other quoted material from a variety of authors. These sources are listed below. In instances where attribution is not directly supplied in the text, the beginning of the quoted material is included.

p. 5   W. G. Sebald, *The Emigrants*, "I did not know what to reply..."

p. 5   John Cage, *M: Writings '67–'72*

p. 6   Robert Creeley, *For Love*

p. 7   Vladimir Nabokov, *Speak Memory*, "Into that arena of radiance..."

p. 7   Stephen Ratcliffe, *More Rocks*

p. 7   Stephen Ratcliffe, *More Rocks*, "stopping to look..."

p. 9   Hui Neng, trans. D. T. Suzuki, *The Zen Doctrine of No Mind*, "the duality of the subject..."

p. 13   Lewis Freedman, *I Want Something Other Than Time*, "The aim of this writing..."

p. 13   Larry Eigner, *Air; the Trees*, "darkness to ripple..."

p. 13   Henry James, *The Golden Bowl*

p. 14   Madeline Gins, *Word Rain*

p. 16.   Nathan Salsburg, *Landwerk*

p. 55   Renee Gladman, *Plans for Sentences,* "These places will let evening glow…"

p. 55   Irma Blank, *Eigenschriften: 1968-1973,* "writing is not linked…"

p. 57   W. G. Sebald, *Vertigo,* "So that instead of drifting into sleep…"

p. 57   Maurice Blanchot, *The Writing of the Disaster,* "But awaiting – just as…"

p. 58   Stanley Cavell, *Little Did I Know: Excerpts from Memory,* "I seem to need some…"

p. 59   Charles Bernstein, *Senses of Responsibility,* "Hope, which is, after all…"

p. 59   Charles Bernstein, *Senses of Responsibility,* "It's not that miracles are achieved…"

p. 62   W. G. Sebald, *Vertigo / The Emigrants,* "It is a fundamentally insane notion…"

p. 70   Marcel Proust, *Remembrance of Things Past,* (Moncrieff translation)

All other quotes are the author's own writing or are sourced from the writing and correspondence of Richard (Rick) Meier, including portions of his books *A Duration* and *A Companion.*

Acknowledgments

Thank you to my editors, Kylan Rice and Lindsey Webb, whose patience and generosity proved indispensable during the development of this book.

Thank you to Lewis Freedman and Richard Meier for providing a shared writing practice in winter 2021. This book germinated from the combinatory texts we assembled at that time.

Thank you to the many friends and family members who are named in this book, and to the numerous others who are unnamed but who are woven into its pages. You have provided community in Marquette, MI; Lake County, IL; Winona, MN; Rainbow Lake, NY; Champaign-Urbana, IL; Chicago, IL; Madison, WI; Milwaukee, WI; Ames, IA; Portland, OR; and all places in between.

An enormous debt of gratitude is owed to Richard Meier and Lisa Fishman, without whom this book would not have reached its final form.

In Memoriam:
Sharon Beth Gray, 1985–2016
Charlie Plescia, 1989–2018
Bradley Swet, 1984–2019

Jordan Dunn is the author of *Physical Geography as Modified by Human Action* (Partly Press) as well as various chapbooks and ephemeral prints including *Common Names, Reactor Woods,* and *A Walk at Doolittle State Preserve*. He lives with his family in Madison, WI, where he edits and publishes Oxeye Press.